BLUE WHEREVER

BLUE WHEREVER

BARRY DEMPSTER

Carolyn Marie Souaid, Editor

EDITIONS

Cover design by Doowah Design.
Cover painting: "Me upon my pony on my boat upon the sea," by Casey McGlynn. Used with permission.
Photo of Barry Dempster by DMN Photo Art.

This book was printed on Ancient Forest Friendly paper.
Printed and bound in Canada by Marquis Book Printing Inc.

We acknowledge the support of The Canada Council for the Arts and the Manitoba Arts Council for our publishing program.

Library and Archives Canada Cataloguing in Publication

Dempster, Barry, 1952–
          Blue wherever / Barry Dempster.

Poems.
ISBN 978-1-897109-39-7

          I. Title.

PS8557.E4827B58 2010   C811'.54   C2010-902182-7

Signature Editions
P.O. Box 206, RPO Corydon, Winnipeg, Manitoba, R3M 3S7
www.signature-editions.com

for Karen

CONTENTS

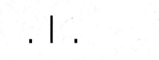

The Gulls

The beach is making big demands today:
sandpapery stench of clams and crabs,
caveman squiggles of gull's feet, greasy-
black dazzle of periwinkles, breeze
like an embrace that has already ended.
And the sand, a billion grains

ever striving to be unique. *See me,*
taste me, feel something crucial going on.
Like a new lover's vast sweep of
confessions, your heart skidding across
the sand, little splashes of joy and horror.
All you can do is walk with your senses

unfastened, daring to be hurt or hailed
at every tide pool, any sand flat.
You begin to bedraggle a bit,
the light fraying away your sunblock,
your camouflage, and you start
to open to the gulls. Curly-headed

rascals, you think, with their boat-like bodies
and crusty feather coats. You'd like to scoop
one up and carry her home under your arms.
But no, she'll have none of that, lumbering
to her feet, backing away like a huge
birdy crab, which still doesn't prepare you

for her raving cry, if cry is what you'd
call it, this hack, sputtering obscenity,
a noise like elevator doors scraping
open, like bridges creaking, like pumps gasping.
It's dirge, and opera, and punk. And it
hates you without regard to good intentions

or poetic haze, whatever you call
yourself at your most vague,

demanding to be left alone
with its hunger and duty.   So
back away, your own sorry imitation
of a crab, even the sand screaming at you,

peerless curses, the periwinkles
soiling the bottoms of your feet.   *Get away
from here*, your admiration has been exposed,
this need to love yourself through words.   *There is
no pretty*, the gulls steam and rattle,
just meat strewn, leaking from shells.

Woodpecker

Today is all about the red-headed woodpecker
on top of the dead tree, knocking itself into dreams.
I shout, toss a stone, even wrap my arms around
the trunk and tug, but nothing changes, *tap, tap, tap,*
incessant, even the grubs can't resist, poking
their white whatevers into the thrust of that
long narrow drill — call it sacrifice or glory.

The real question is *what*, not *how*. The grief
that I hold grave in my heart, spend my days trying
to resolve. What if I gave the same attention
to happiness, would I find it somewhere
in the queer ridges of my nails or the
stringy backs of my shins? Decide to live on
love alone and I'd either starve or conjugate,
a little fondness joined to same until the sighs
begin to sound like bells, giddy with momentum.

Make me as tenacious as a woodpecker,
knocking myself out on requited things. This
forest walk, for example, no longer just *through*,
but *amidst*. Trees linking arms and leaning in.
I count up to seven squirrels and then I add
myself, another flourish. Each of us,
alone, together, losing track of bitterness,
tapping a simple not-so-secret code.

How Many Atoms Can One Man Hold?

Today, my arms shoot out in front of me
as I'm strolling down the street, savouring
the lustre of April heat, tiny
spots of green floating in my eyes.
Like Frankenstein suddenly jolted
into life, there I am, groping
the air, gathering it in my fists
like a lover's hair. Do I squeeze too hard?
All that empty space, begging to be held.

Kora at two, asked to hug a tree,
flinging herself at opportunity,
laying her plushy cheek against the bark.
The ghost of my father constantly
touching everything, from crumpled
coffee cups to the lips of purple
crocuses, his lack of fingers
overflowing with waves of light.
And that cardinal skid-landing on
a cedar branch, clasping its bit of
lust, its proper piece of planet.

It hurts to stretch myself into
all these other shapes, but the day
demands it. The pull in my back
as I lift a globe of leaves, slipping
them safely in a bag's embrace.
The way my wrists spark when I'm
carrying electricity from room to room.

How many atoms can one man hold
before the world starts to spill?
Today, I keep piling them on,
armfuls of April breeze, with dust so fine
it feels like a cape of silk.
The cardinal and I succumb to the same
tang of cedar. His wings, my fingers,
touching for an instant, lifting air.

River Rocks

Hoisting river rocks at *Farmer Jack's*,
80-pound bags destined for my garden,
a 20-foot strip where the rain never reaches
and even the hardiest perennial droops.
First bag, my back clutches a ball of pain;
second, tears some actual muscle.
But by the third, I am the ache,
the all of us inseparable,
rock dust coating my aura,
lending me a ghostly gleam.

I like to think of them as lifted from
the Bow, perhaps a nook of beach in Banff.
But northern Ontario makes more sense,
a fast flow giving groove
to an insubstantial shoreline.
Moose have probably stepped on some,
hooves tottering.
Raccoons washing their faces, tiny drips
darkening the surface to a black pearl.
Maybe even a suicidal salmon, one ill-timed leap.

Now the only creatures that they'll see
will be neighbourhood cats searching
for a place to piss.
And me, playing stepping stones in the moonlight
when it's too late to tell the difference
between a coneflower and a weed.
Will they feel purposeless, even dislocated?
A whim, perhaps, to think they can feel at all.
Imagine, a 20-foot strip of sheer longing,
almost half a ton of hard regrets.

I wonder if mankind invented feelings
as a kind of pretend: I love
therefore I'm better than a river rock,
less susceptible to fate.

But then someone steals your heart,
tosses it in the air
before throwing it to the distance;
nothing to do but lie
where it lands and blend in.
How inhuman resiliency can be.

Most summer mornings you can find me
watering the river rocks.
Not that the attention matters,
or that devotion is even healthy,
but just in case.
Today I introduced them to some ladybugs,
wishing they could fall in love,
wear their bliss like little drops of blood.
But they're being secretive, pretending
the inanimate way is holy,
a stunning coldness in the place of eyes.

Swoop

You pay more attention to a dozen eggs
than you do the cedar waxwings
flourishing their bright yellow fans.
The front window is full of them
as you vacuum the invisible, straighten
the pillows for the third time in one afternoon.
Lift your head from those nests
of duty, whip the Windex bottle from your hand
and throw it at the hallway mirror.
The birds are bobbing on the branches
of the mountain ash, little caramel whisks
of hairdo above Lone Ranger masks.
Remember when you planted it; who could love
those orange berries more than you?
Almost flowers, you said. But that was
before you lost yourself in straightening pictures,
in dried weed arranging. Before your eyes
got too busy searching for dust.
The cedar waxwings are high-wiring,
shaking those thin red stripes
on their tail feathers. If you could just resist
lining the garbage can with yesterday's news,
struggling to remember. If you could stop yourself
believing that only e-mails fly. Look at the way
their tawny throats quiver as they swallow each feast.
How they slip sometimes and almost turn
into hummingbirds, perfecting mid-air. For the love
of loftiness, give that teapot a break. Hang up
the phone, quit revising. One of them
is about to crash into the window, a surprising
thump for a creature so stuffed with breeze.
You owe the sky a little something
for not tearing off your roof, for allowing you
to hunker down around your evening grace.
Can't you see that the outside world
is showing off for a reason, that the berry swoop
is the best thing to do with a pair of wings?

No Time

— for Carol Gall

It's that time again, the world
speeding on its downturn spin;
leaves with blood in their faces
growing dizzy and letting go,
sky shifting skins.   Time to

cancel the garden, call it *heaps*
or *ruins*, something other
than faith and flourish.
The Muskoka chairs are heavy
but allow themselves to be

hauled into the garage.
The black hose uncoils and
empties, wrapped back up again
and tossed in a corner
with the watering cans.

It's all summer stuff,
trinkets and tools, things to
balance blossoms, strings and poles,
sprinklers and little rusted spades.
It's time to set the rakes dancing,

swell the paper bags, sprinkle
sweat and seed.   Believe that
the spin continues, November
climbing the shadow of May.
And as for you and your hibernation

fantasy, get over it, someone has to
pry open a door and shovel
a crooked path, otherwise the clocks
will stick, the calendars just hang there.
Pick yourself up, flakes of leaves

snagged in your sweater,
tote a hug of wood, wrap the roses,
sing a slow but heartfelt dirge.
It's time to tilt your head back
and watch snow spilling from those

cold bins of cloud, squash a hat
over your own coldness and run
for the cover of a window
where you can wave to grass
before it goes under.   It's almost

no time again, that season where
even words freeze, pens casting
blue sleep on white pages
the way the dead still carry colour
in their folded wrists.

Happy To Be Cold

This year is trapping me in despair,
so agrees the robin pacing across
the frozen grass, trying to talk herself
into a taste for frozen worms.
The ladybug echoes her impatience, one
shocking drop of blood in the April snow.
How can I manage to be happy in all this
desolation? Happiness is the whole point
if you're a human being. Happy
to be cold and lonely, to be unloved.

Hard times, I thin myself to a shadow,
the vague hint of footsteps behind my
friend's back, the faintest flicker at the
fireplace. Not even war can stop me from
loving the world, quietly unrequited.
The killer virus shrinks at the very mention
of *quarantine*. The tulip shoots shiver with
purpose. Cold and cruel, a chorus
complaint. Just touching a chair
these days is a kind of embrace.

If only I could find a quorum of buds
willing to open despite this frozen dread.
Or persuade that robin to hop inside,
warm herself in the oak wood glow.
Maybe then my friend would shut
down the pain, turn around
and step into my shadow.

Moths

Ariel is crazy for the moths,
her own private paw-swatting party,
skidding around the house, leaving
dusty streaks on the kitchen floor.
Before I start bragging about
her feline prowess, I remind myself

that she's killing them, her purr raunchy
as a machine gun. When she leaps
onto my lap, she leaves little goo stains
on my shorts, her whiskers laden
with what might be entrails. And here
I thought mothballs were cruel.

I even turn off lamps when wings
begin circling the bright idea of
martyrdom. It seems to be my job
to keep everything alive: spiders
flitting in my fist, a wasp trapped
inside a juice glass, a cricket

packed carefully in a Kleenex.
No way am I participating
in doom. What do I do about
Ariel and her bloody instincts?
Hoist her to my knee and tell her tales
of cats sealed in Egyptian tombs

with nothing to eat but death itself?
How to scare the animal out of her?
Bodies are wriggling wildly
in every room, thrusting against
panic. Amazing how much strength in one
desperate breeze, that will to continue.

I crawl after Ariel's crawling
like a caricature of the conscience
she doesn't have.   And am rewarded
in my sleep with a tiny pair
of powdery wings one flutter
faster than the end of all dreams.

Blindness

The barn is ripe with geldings and mares;
how well they get along without
the bother of balls and fidelity.
The one stallion snorts by the far door,
as if disgusted by the easy
equanimity, knocking the gate
with his hammer hooves, letting everyone
know they're unsafe. A sheen of nervousness
in the air, flecks of hay drifting
in the sliced sunbeams like tiny flares.
Except for Sprout, across the way,
one of the castrati, whose head-bends
beg a bold friendliness. From the left,
he's suede and apple butter, with
an emperor's snout, a profile
fit for a coin. But seen from the right,
he becomes a missing eye, a long-
ago accident, as if a cage
had lost its golden bird, or a shrine
its simple saint. Gruesome, perverse,
the worst thing you'll see today. Wouldn't
blame you if you ran, muck flicking
from the soles of your shoes. But of course,
you'll stay, the empty socket of your will
reminding you of how distorted
you often feel. Just your heart
alone is an ugly mess;
if anyone ever really took the time
for a good look. And so you ease closer,
Sprout nodding, urging you in. He breathes
the back of your neck, then lowers himself
into a nuzzle, left side first, then
right, oh, Christ, here it comes, the accident
that never ends, the loneliness that
reminds you how much you need to be seen.
The barn goes dark and light in separate
strips, a pattern you'd once have thought

was choice.   This time though you touch it all,
the bronze flanks, the shady fringe of mane,
the nothingness that narrows to
an incandescent finger, finally
entering the loss.   Sprout whinnies,
less alone now, as close to loved
as shock can get.   You stake a foothold
in the straw and shit, and stare up at him,
all flinches fled.   Blindness, so soft
and eager, it almost talks.

Dianthus

We sneaked into the churchyard while the service
was hankering after holiness, most of the high notes
split down the spine like pecans. I wish I could say
we were after the same forgiveness, that we'd spotted
God amongst the dianthus, but no, it was the flowers
that drew us through the low-slung wrought iron gate,
the colour pink in profusion, a blast of it. We wanted
a touch, not the flowers themselves, their nubby little
blooms and grey-green stalks, but the colour, the pink,
how it matched the tones of our skin as we reached out
to pat it, to feel it leap into the monkey creases of our palms.
It tickled, with the slightest suggestion of a burn, energies
mingled. Inside the church, a sermon droned colourless.
While in the garden, there was barely the sound of dianthus
being stroked, of lesser and greater pinks devising
a relationship. I'm not saying God was anywhere
in the vicinity; after all, Sunday mornings are his time
to steer the world alone, all the mortals busy with their
dallying songs. But something — stems, petals, spaces
between our fingers where the blossoms popped through —
was telling the truth, was all it needed to be, a temporary
faith. We tiptoed away from the church as another hymn was
tuning up, shiny hands hidden like stolen gifts behind our backs.

Blue Wherever

In the new world, my cat doesn't go mad,
her swampy pupils shrinking to pebbles,
her nightly howls tuned down to a purr.
And the three-year-old niece of a friend
snaps back to life, *sudden unexplained death*
just a particularly bad dream.
The cottage roof bellows a deep breath
and stops leaking. The mouldy pita
shrugs off its green dots. This headache
I've been hosting for days suddenly lifts,
a spaceship spinning from my brain.

And all that predictable stuff: no more war,
hunger, loneliness or the need to write a poem
like this. May love finally whoop. May
sex slip into the keen darkness like an after-
dinner mint. No more mean or morbidly
obese, not a trace of penury or objectification.
May the headlines be mistaken for cheers.
May the heavens pour with honey, angel bees
slid beneath our tongues like hit songs.

In this state of perfection, we wake up
to a bone ark bobbing on a blue wherever,
just the two of us in our various roles.
The doves will come and go, their breeze
adding frills to the blunt tops of waves.
The elephants, surprisingly, can swim.
As can the caramel-coloured ants
with their hollow abdomens. And those
who can't, well, they will ride
the slopes of our floating shoulders,
almost in the shapes of wings.

Pastoral

Three deer amidst the haycocks,
a buck and two does, oh, so pastoral
and chummy, not even the breeze of our
brakes elicits more than a tall-ear twitch.

But later, darkness broken into pieces
of a dozen different puzzles,
a lone deer tries to leap the highway
just a few feet in front of us, darting

death with hardly a breath to spare, a stunt
of faith. And I think about the gun blasts
I'd been listening to all day and can't
understand the nonchalance in the field,

how those three knew we were harmless, mere
admirers. As for the one almost
wrecked by a thwack of headlights, what was
she desiring — didn't she realize

our penchant for getting in the way of
instinct and gentleness? Here I go,
idealizing the beasts again, I
know, disowning my humanness. As if

I had a tiny tail curled up
against the seat of my spine. Do the deer
live with a forgiveness we can't begin
to fathom? Did they recognize a

carful of innocence, a wise sixth sense,
or was their very presence a willingness
to die for our formidable sins?
The doe we almost hit offered herself

full-bodied, sacrifice at its most
naked and alive. All we could do
was swerve, a clumsy shift in the divine,
as if angels were just lucky guys.

Wallop

The wind is shaking the dickens
out of oak leaves, crashing them
to the cemetery lawn. It's
beating up on squirrels, whipping
their tails into frenzies,
flinging acorn lids in their faces
like high-tech frisbees. Bled rose
petals and pine cones fly by,
wreaths torn to pieces. Is that
a weapon or a starling
that has closed its wings and become
pure speed? Even the clouds are soaring,
grey Sunday hats hell-bent out of shape.

God knows what's it doing to me,
my smile stretched to a slingshot,
my eyes thrown open like
patio doors. I look like a
cartoon version of Munch's *Scream*.
But I love the wildness, the elements.
I'm having trouble sucking in
that wallop of air, not breathing
out again, holding the moment
steady, one blow away from a gasp.

And inside? Are the dead shivering
in their subway-train coffins,
is motion without muscle
like being out of control?
The wind has no boundaries.
It shakes up your secret places,
those mistresses of fate, leaves you
unsure which is fantasy and
which is just a long, long wait.
It turns you into a squirrel,
a black flicker of crazy tail.

Relentless

Spindly thing, mosquito with a red light
bulb in its belly, prowling the dashboard
in search of an even thicker fix.
Angel of Death shrunk to the prick
of a needle. Wireless disease.
You stab at it with a Kleenex,
queasy self-preservation, but it
skitters safely into an air vent.
Won't be long before you're slapping
every surface, panic's empty fist.
You can feel it injecting your ankles,
infiltrating your underpants.
Might as well crash the car, surrender
to the tiny David of its courage.
It will rise from the smoking metal
with a splash of your own blood.

Accident, With Warbler

A singular morning, from the candy-striper
viscera of a blossom, to the beige-bodied
daddy-long-legs with the Folies-Bergère black stockings,
all sorts of firsts: crown jewels worn once on their way
to display. So when the warbler soars into our
windshield, I know I'm mere accompaniment,
a few tears mixed in a feather stew, but can't stop
wondering where the rest of the tune was heading.
A surge of wantonness, a splurge of air currents
overlapping, swirling fiddlesticks of beak and feet
trying to figure themselves out. One warbler,
primo uomo, one dark flight. One voice slashed
on glass, a smear under a microscope.
One moment of chill blast in the never-quite-like-
this June sky, as if an icicle had been dropped
twirling into a heatwave, two clattering notes,
a splatter of clear, fused light.

Coyote

After a grease feast at Wendy's, I no longer
believe that food is a synonym for nourishment.
A ketchup stain on my left thigh
shaped like an island nation, someplace
hopeless.   A piece of gristle between my teeth
like a second tongue.   So preoccupied that at first
the coyote in the parking lot seems
unreal, an escaped cartoon from a kid's place mat,
some hamburglar or combo creature.   I point
and laugh, almost leaning in to pat him, until
he growls as if a toy truck were stuck in his throat.
Whoa, bubbles from my giant Coke back up.
As real as it's going to get tonight.   He paws
a little further, presses his stingy flanks
against a blue Mazda's front bumper, looks as if
he's going to lift his leg.   *Ugly* is all I can think:
hips higher than belly, head tucked in at the chin,
strings of grey-black fur glued across his spine.
Waiting for a handout, I suppose, an overflowing
garbage can, too needy to last until dark.
I seriously consider returning inside,
ordering him "the works," tossing it
piece by juicy piece into his dark jaws.
Offering him a home, three squares,
a scummy water dish, and a rug beside my bed.
Maybe even love, if that isn't going too far,
mine the only human hand allowed to scratch
behind his ear.   We could be real together, man
and whatever he'd like to be called, a twosome,
a partnership — hanging out in parking lots,
sniffing ketchup stains.   Who knows how far
I'd have gone if a happy family hadn't barged out
the restaurant door, squealing *Coyote*, sending him
loping into the field behind us like a cloud of dust.
Soon, I'll be alone again with my
plastic stomach and greasy fingerprints, patting
the car keys in my otherwise empty pocket.

A Shooing

Heading for the garage, I'm flummoxed
by a sudden flux of wings, a shooing
I suppose, a good old-fashioned scold.
It takes a second for the flurry

to become a robin, and then another
to spot the nest tucked in the climbing
hydrangea. Time goes haywire after this:
blue egg smash-ups on boyhood sidewalks,

once an actual chick, bald and wet,
like a template for a horror cartoon.
A former me with a lit firecracker
in my fingers and visions of a cooked bird.

Cheering my fat cat, Rusty, with his mouthful
of beak and fluff. Call it sport, call it
ignorance, imagine what I might have done
to Icarus, or some rare angel on a

whimsy trip, the air a scald of smoke and
feathers? Still the predator, the robin
bawling another round. How do I say
reformed in bird-speak? Will waving a white

Kleenex do? Not as safe as I'd like to think.
I'm already plotting the stepladder
and a closer look, almost reaching out
and in, one small soft stroke. I wasn't all bad

back then, did my share of saving sparrows
and finches, matchboxes lined with cotton
batting, and worms I'd chase down with a
coffee spoon. I could be benevolent, add

some twigs where the wind gets through, send
my current cat sprawling with a well-placed spank.

If only the robin would trust me, stop flying
in my face.   If only I could eke out

a little fatherhood, name the trio of
tykes, clean up the lice, savour the breeze.
Is it narcissistic to want a
personal relationship with everything?

I stand outside the garage flapping my arms,
tipping my heels an inch off the grass,
one of the lofty, the forgiven few.   This
is flight, I announce to a sky full of wings.

Temporary, A Lament

Mist rises off the hyped green lawn
like a side effect, the morning sickly —
a headache of grey clouds. Buddha says
to love this too, every microcosm,
let the clammy seep through your bones
on its way to the soaked absolute.
And so you wring yourself dry again
and again, a pink washcloth smothering
a fever. You welcome the possibility
of flood, the entire planet
flowing through in soggy twosomes,
from earthworms with their liquid wriggles,
to those raindrops in the shapes of wrens.
You keep an open mind about everything,
enter the mist as it's entering you.

Later, the day finally repainted, you
drag a deck chair to the delphiniums
to snatch some sun, realizing
that this too is only passing through.
Buddha giggles the love word again.
With him, it feels like you're supposed to
lie there and let yourself be fondled and stroked.
Something is tickling your balls, no, wait,
it's your earlobe, and it's more like a scrape.
You're definitely a bottom, six feet under
all the blooms of mist, all the sun-strings
tying themselves to meaningless breezes.

Just once you'd like to reach up out of yourself
and hold on, like a kid squeezing a balloon
as it shape-shifts towards emptiness. Grab
the mist by the back of its straggly neck.
Slip a finger into a crack of sun
until it expands into a full-fledged flame.
Be bold, be possessive, tie Buddha into
knots, say *no, you're meant to be mine.* Of course,

this will achieve nothing but misery,
but your misery nonetheless. You and it
can sit under the moon tonight, the sky
offering no commitments. Call it friendship,
dialogue, or heavy petting. It will feel
sublime for moments out of time. And then
it will feel reneged, like nakedness
wrapped in the robes of a shooting star.

Animalia

He has feelings for snakes: tiny quibbles
of affection coiling around his pleasure points
like white mice. Endearments every bit as
domestic as father and son — *my little grass,*
my sweet water moccasin — rising all the way
to respect, *king cobra* sung in the shape of
a kowtow, *anaconda* stretching his throat
to a four-lane artery. Sinewy, agile
feelings, but nothing close to adoration,
no sweat pools in his palms, no breath racing
after something to breathe on, no taste buds
popping open like just-baked poems.

Plenty of inclination to keep his heart
spinning (hamster-ish). In fact, he's stumped to think
of even one creature he doesn't sort of like.
Flamingos, for example, shrimp-pink and
pouting in the hot sun. They tickle him silly,
as if his blood had sprouted feathers. Cows, too,
mooing in the muck, the black of their silent movie eyes
titillating in a butter sculpture kind of way.

You can't even spook him with roaches or rats,
he's tender to the scuttle, survival's erotics,
the raw energies that keep plasma in its place.
He'll let you in on a secret: *Even humans,*
especially those two X chromosomes dabbed
behind opalescent ears. Always good for
a rush, nerves sliding down his spine.
Nothing he enjoys more than a crowd
of them, lots of snuggle and adrenaline,
ankles lifted, necks folded into
Virgin Mary wonder. P.S.
the apes and baboons stir up similar
flavours; he can't always tell them apart.

But all this watching chafes his will, reducing
him to a trickle. A bear, a dragonfly,
a blonde, too much chance and
wildness. This is when he skins the sky
and plops his elbows on the table. *Bring me
a goddamned cat*, he cries. A gingery squirm of
coat and muscle, ice pick paws and snit-quick eyes,
and with a tail that wraps around the world
like a leather belt cutting off the blood supply.
Ah, that purr falling into a flush of
selfishness no other living thing can fathom.
His knuckles ache with longing, true love arching
its broken hips. *Look at her.* See how
she refuses to look back, or if she does,
it's just to gauge the whereabouts of that
white mouse of pleasure bounding inside.

Before The Sweetness Is Crushed

It's May and the trees are gussying up
with little thread-balls of blossoms,
the kind of corsages a 6-year-old
girl would wear to match the dandelions
behind her ears. Also, magnolias,
a case of pink flutters so serious
bees are buzzing *Pomp and Circumstance*.
But my favourite is the willow —
embraceable blonde — as if a rich man
had bought up all the world's golden hair,
draped it over his arms.

What's that you're wearing, a swirl skirt
and a tight denim blouse? What kind of tree
would you be if your skin were just
a little rougher and the soles
of your feet owned the ground? Today,
I ogled a slinky cherry
on Bathurst, pastels soft as
baby antlers, and a real swing
to the way she let the breeze divide her.
I still can't stop coveting, catching
the petals before their sweetness is crushed.

There's a reason you won't stand naked
before me, terrified of newness,
how it exposes everything maimed and lost,
how it warps desire into greed. Poor you,
clutching your clothes like ragged bits of leaf,
actually managing to feel concealed.
I'd rather love a beech tree, tawny
and bejewelled, shedding its inhibitions, coin
by coin, until the only thing left to spend
is its splendor, bare branches
giving nestle to the sun.

Just A Tree

That tree outside your window
starts out as just a tree,
a maple of some ilk, big and bushy,
divided into tiers of glisten.
Okay, there is no such thing
as just a tree, what was I thinking?
It was storied and flashy right from
the beginning, a burst of *look at me*.
And so we do, talking
our relationship into an empty corner,
until no nakedness remains.
We talk from the roots up, confess
things we can't tell one another,
intimacies that fly into the stretched-full
branches, bold and bloodied as cardinals.
Somewhere in the thick, a rudimentary nest
where my heart pretends to be an egg.
When the street lamps snap on, I am lifted
from the couch, tipped across the window sill,
reeled into a scurry of stem-pierced light.
And you, what losses have you hidden
in this blur of green, what parts
of your body feel as defensive as twigs?

When The Snowflakes

You know you're alive
when the snowflakes start to sting,
especially those that land
on the dimpled creases of your neck.
As if the heavens were bombarding you,
angels with soft rocket launchers
cradled under wings.
You on Bloor Street, under
full attack. Someone is liable
to mistake you for a snowman,
stick a carrot up your nose.

Other sensible folk bundled in
scarves or draped in shadowy hoods
rush by between flakes, avoiding
gazes, as socially awkward as the undead.
A woman who'd be pretty
if she were really flesh and blood
sails past with a gleam in her eyelashes.
And the lover of the man whose hair
has turned completely white
will mistake him for a strange new loneliness.
But the one you're most drawn to
is the savage adolescent, his head
thrown back, tongue stuck out,
one sizzle after another.

It's all too much, ducking into doorways,
wishing stores would stay
open, give back a little solace.
But it turns out the merchandise
is too smart to expose itself —
it knows how to master nonchalance
as the skies fall down around it.
No whiff of perfume or cashmere glove
is in danger of freezing to death.
Even the bread in the shutdown bakery

is safely growing a day older.

And so you step back out
on the slushy street, surrendering
yourself to the air.   Instantly sheathed
in cold, baby hairs on the sheen
of your face tied into little knots.
Let January have its twisted way with you —
go on, bare head, tongue, the whole war chest.

.2.

Love The View

The houses sit like stepping clouds
across a celestial strait.
Trimmed-poodle bungalows.
Families time-lapsing as they scoot
across the universe.

Air so thin it's anaesthetic.
Somewhere along the way
I spilled my self,
sliding down a chimney, splayed out
on the hearth like a novelty rug.
Suburban privilege: learning
to love the view, the leaping legs of
strangers on their way to paradise.

No spot quite so ingenuous
as mid-air, just bobbing,
too far from the rest of the world
to care.
A pet apple tree in the front yard
frolicking into blossom once a year.
And always the hope that someone else
might swoon in exactly the same way.

The dawns and dusks up here
croon. We are spaced out
and happy, hovering on
white sofas, fingers stirring
whirlpools on windowpanes,
drawing Van Gogh ties
for the man in the moon.

Mid-Life Crisis

He comes to fetch me in a Mercedes Benz,
the moneybags equivalent of a comb-over
or a blonde. He gives me a minute to grapple
with envy, then peels back the roof —
a convertible no less. I think swank thoughts
and then stop thinking at all. We both forget
Edmonton — the wind pure force, dividing our brains
into tracks, each one leading somewhere bright and
meaningless. We tear past streets and parking lots,
heading for highway the way gods used to hanker
after myth. Of course, this attracts attention:
women at bus stops bending into the breeze,
seeing sultry versions of themselves in the steel.
Did I mention the car is the same shade
as cherries soaked in vodka? No one notices
a fleeting thing like age, hair flying off our heads —
we're simplified, all flash and speed.

Long Weekend

What did I do with the days?
Sprinkled them with talc, drank
to happier ways, wrote them
in my notebook for future spec.
I combed my hair, at least a dozen times,
especially when the rain
did its plastering gig.
I puttered about the garden,
shooting weeds, whispering invocations
to the dirt, did all sorts of silly things,
from naming my new spruce Cedric
to gobbling too much Thai.
Ordinary days, slippages,
hardly holiday fare, this bit of winter
in May, stats showing the superiority
of times past. Then sleep,
don't let me forget the zzz's,
as many of them as good intentions.
I cleaned out my closet, unkinked
the cat, leaned into fate with what
I hoped was a flexible stance.
I yanked, I drove, I telephoned,
all the while feeling incomplete.
Were the hours simply to be spent?
Those infamous *shoulds* drilling their greys,
piling lesser with regrets. I should have
unravelled the brute truth, baffled
the chronic *too*, written a template
for the perfect poem. Should have spun
the days into sacrifice and myth, something
easily mistaken for accomplishment.

Tacky

Christmas tacky in the daylight —
Gloria Swanson's close-up
at the end of *Sunset Boulevard*.
A four-foot plastic Santa tied
to a front yard pine by yellow twine,
coerced to spread his kidnapped hope.
And good old Frosty in a giant bubble
like one of those snowstorm paperweights,
a smile slashed where his lips should be.
Grazing nearby, a pair of white wire reindeer
and a rather dog-like polar bear
giving the food chain a discomfiting revision.
Even in the woods today, a runt spruce hung with
three red and silver balls, as if Mother Nature
had gone to Wal-Mart for that extra touch.

At the travel clinic, an artificial tree
brushes against the ceiling, a strewn copy
of Maclean's underneath passing itself
off as a gift. Across the reception window,
a string of sparkly cards, greetings
from tropical islands, I imagine. When the doctor
arrives with his bright handful of needles,
I think of tinsel pouring into my veins, blood
blossoming into puffy little bows.
Tetanus, Typhoid, Hep A,
like reindeer names. The new holes
in my arms seasonally rosy.

Come night, the magic shimmers, making
me forget how puny spirit can be.
I stand out on the lawn, drenched
in light, a North Star of a man
pointing a path to paradise. Even Frosty
is lit up like an angel. Times like these
can only be believed in the dark
when snow is the colour of a rainbow.

Hydrangea

The hydrangea enters the house
in a bubble of cellophane,
blue-mauve hairdo intact.

All the trouble nature takes
to divide crocuses from hyacinths,
daffodils from tulips, assigning

tones as if they were birthstones,
a certain glint of blonde, an outright
orange, a black-tinged red.

Are we to feel the same
focus, each with our
two hands and ten fingers?

Is the bump of your brow the only
way the hydrangea can tell us apart?
If the garden were given a pair of us,

we'd stand side by side, same page
in the anatomy book, same bleaching
under the sun, same midnight cries.

Stripped of bows and string, we'd be
a sorry sight, not near as proud
as that Easter lily measuring itself

in layers of cream. We'd never share a pot
so naturally, all that ingrained fear. No one
would ever hand us to a lover as a gift.

Office Party

A seasonal spread: pizza, fajitas, ribs,
steaming in silver dishes,
Oh, to stick something
appropriate in our mouths, step back
and watch the office shimmy.

Naked Santa screen savers.
Costume jewellery
dipping into secretaries' breasts,
all that diversionary bling.

Look at the way the guy from
Sales, the one with bangs,
periscopes as he bends down
to retrieve the receptionist's serviette.

And the girl from Billing (we all belong,
just somewhere else) sucking on
whole ice cubes, pretending
big mouth is a talent.

A woman in red holds out a greasy set of fingers.
How about a kiss? asks the talking mistletoe.

Elsewhere in the room a lonely man
longs for another, a wife wishes
her husband loved her more and knew her less.

While the poet in the corner, probably
a temp, discovers words are barely
able to describe let alone seduce.
I like your hair, he thinks, then revises.
I like how it would fall across my face.

Monster

Man in his early 50's out for a walk.
Apple face. Runners and puffy jacket.
The bare trees seem to like him.

He belongs, hallelujah, the grass
cushy with his footprints, the sky
a benevolent shade of blue.

Until (and here's where the story goes
strange), he overtakes a slightly bedraggled
thirty-something mom and her kids.

Overtakes sounds aggressive, I know,
but it's the only word that describes
the way her mouth pinches into

an Edvard Munch while her eyes
light matches in some unseen dark.
She clutches her daughters, screaming —

how dare you overtake us! —
or would have had he not pushed through
with a startling *Hey, is this a beautiful*

day or what? Walking on, he wonders
who he'd been in her frightened eyes,
what he was capable of.

Dismemberment, now there's a shot
at self-esteem. Just think,
he could be burying bodies right now

instead of feeling like a pariah.
He rolls across the street on his two
cumbersome balls, coughing a little warning

to the old woman he's just about
to *overtake*, her fear already
wiping his hands of blood.

Wastelands

We drive through wastelands, chronic
vistas of strip malls and construction sites,
wind-drummed parking lots and townhouse
jungles. Wheeling our way to a poetry café,
you'd think the scenery would make
a better effort, offer up some snappy graffiti,
an eyesore worth the stanza space. But
it's all highway simmer, grey clutching
grey, big box stores mooing in the distance.
Asked again, would I still choose poetry,

or steer for something that could make
a difference: landscape artist or
demolition man? Is there such a job
as Commissioner of Ugliness?   Motels
with their *V's* collapsed. Factory windows
so dirty only Superman could peer inside.
We drive on through the blight.
Perhaps we should have stayed home, read
our poems in hushed tones, watched the alphabet
perform its prettiest garden poses.

But we're brave as eyeballs can be,
filling our prisms with plastic bags
hanging from half-dead trees, with rubber
roadkill and enough steel glare
to jolt every sorry crow from its love of shadow.
We're sucking in the urban sprawl, the horror
of all our worst mistakes. Surely, a poem
will be waiting at the end of the smear,
a pothole deep enough to hold two poets
and their enormously optimistic pens.

Library Book Sale

At first glance, the sale
is a swath of chaos, all those
rumoured-to-be-lost words
laid out in their innate fluorescence.
Tables marked *Fiction*, *Sports*,
Celebrities, as if the literate life
were a board game, every square
with its own story.
Draw closer.   The paperback romances
heave paragraphs into waves of pages.
And the thrillers with their chilled psychopaths
like something so furred in the freezer
you can't remember what it once was.
The *Self-Help* sign promises a kit
and a tiny tube of glue: how to lose
50 pounds in 20 minutes, how to get
a head, suck a million, rid the world
of pestilence and regrets.
Where should you leave this poem
when it's finished?   You can't find
Poetry, and although *Literature*
certainly has room, it feels
presumptuous.   You've already missed
most of your life in *Miscellaneous*.
Fact is, somewhere in here, a book
is calling you by name.   Alphabetical
just a synonym for belonging.

If I Can Dance

Muscle-strained thighs ache
to shake loose, reconnect to hips.

Dance diagnostic: my body a blueprint
of sway and groove, a little orchestra

jamming in my chest, slamming/swishing,
blood swirling in an upside-down tambourine.

To hell with child pose or eagle flying,
this new oomph is a goose with clothespins

on its wings, a major wriggle.
A lima bean one simmer away

from shedding its skin. A strutting slinky
down red castle stairs. Heel/toe,

heel/toe. If I can dance in yoga class,
I'll glue my heart back together,

get high on the fumes. Be able to loom,
or levitate, enough heft to lift harmony,

the white page beneath the black notes.
Able to cry, kvetch, even calculate,

cut the need to fill myself with nothing
but belly breath. Quickly, before the flutes

barge in and the music goes all
mountainy, I shimmy to my soles,

cock and balls like Motown puppets,
trombones of my arms tossed into the air

tension released. There, dancing man,
chakras swung wide, energy pouring across the floor.

How To Fall

Nothing is happening — might as well
have wrapped myself in newsprint
and stowed away under the stairs.
The house squats on its haunches
while the yard's in a fog, garden
half-dead, blossoms reduced to
shrunken heads. And the sky
lays down a concrete slab
over the mouth of a well.
Even the fuck-all squirrels
are in hiding.

Nothingness has a way of
maddening the make-do gods
who prefer stunts and other forms
of group denial. Let's see — they could
cut loose my neighbour's toy dog,
overfill the atmosphere with snarls
as small as pubic hairs. Or they
could flip out — crash a truck
through my back fence, a load of
carrots tumbling into an orange
inferno. They could even mess
with me, knock me out
like a pine plank's knot.

In the end, one god is all it takes,
the one with the nimblest fingers
pinching free the last oak leaf on the tree,
spinning it in a cradle of idle air,
a lilt to the left, a swing to the right,
slow-motion drift — lessons on how
to fall, to suddenly be everything.
When it finally lands, the grass
grows an inch of welcome mat

and all the husks rustle together
a little cheer. Then the house
tilts just enough to spit me
from my nothing perch, insisting
that I too try to make a difference.

Unnatural

The rectory garden looks very English,
tangled with forget-me-nots and bleeding hearts,
the blues and reds doing their best to get along,

a cultivated democracy, complete with
pots of annuals reminding us that not
everything lovely lasts.   When I first spot

the teddy bear leaning against the pale leaves
of a clematis, I think abandonment,
a crying, rose-cheeked child,

but then I realize it's decoration,
like the sequined humming birds
in my own back yard, like the earring in my

left lobe, like the fantasy life shadowing
my dailiness when facts aren't good enough.
The new pornography of TV decorating

shows, cookbook covers glistening with sugar glaze,
fashion magazines where cheekbones are
Waterford crystal.   Fancy it, a flourish,

glitter in the genes.   On a Newmarket stroll,
I came across a garden filled with kitsch, from
Wonder Woman dolls to Dinky Toys, finger

puppets to plastic clowns, all frolicking amongst
the hostas, equal rights to splendor.
Is there a health store product called

Natural Beauty or am I just being
nostalgic, missing the simple things?
Should I splurge and add doilies

to my yarrow, frills to my foxglove?
Oh, the ornament fatigue, the orange lily
gilded to death with an umpteenth coat of gold.

It takes an act of will not to scoop up that teddy bear
and track down a playground. *Frou-Frou Bandit Strikes Again,*
I can picture the headlines.

Itching to get home to my plain bathroom mirror,
strip off my disguise, rip out my earring,
be as unnatural as only naked can.

Little Voice

Tripping the ups and downs of Concession 2, head wedged in a cloud
(a daydream guillotine), I hear his voice for the first time today: *Get a
load of the view.* His eyeballs are sitting on the dash, gold as roadside
grass with a hint of shucked October blue. All of it — the stripped
cornfield, strewn gravel from the reservoir parking lot, *For Sale* signs
outside the country bungalows — needs to be admired, will turn
invisible if one more guy drives by dazed. He throws his voice out the
window, ready to name wherever it lands.

◆

You know the feeling, not only someone watching you, but another
look inside your own looking. You snag a hard-boiled egg from its hot
water and for a second, snatched by a sunbeam, it becomes a Fabergé.
The way the black cat's fur floats in the air like miniature kittens. Your
wife's scribble of a smile, a secret code a more obsessed man would have
solved.

◆

For awhile I called him Jesus, then Buddha, growing woozier every
day. How about Hermes, or Vulcan? Or something plain, like Joe?
Not even God can make me grandiose anymore. A tiny oomph and I
whisper, *You.* Nada. *Friend, buddy, hey fella.* Cloaked in silence from
ears to toes. Maybe I'm really all alone, an imaginary imagination.
Wait, was that a groan?

◆

You know what it's like to wake up feeling worth it: another sunrise
in the jewellery drawer, heart and lungs staying put, a half-full jar of
champagne honey in the fridge, plans for an orgasm before your feet
hit the floor. That voice that oozes, *Lucky*, that helps you forget the
Hydro bill, the dentist's reamer, the blue timer ticking inside your wrist.
You stretch the bed's warmth longer, wider, the last dream growing
thinner and wavier like a bubble blown from a plastic pipe. *Pop*, he
says.

I call it *Chocolate*, he corrects me, *Yum*. Words are flukes, is what I think he's trying to say, ways of stalling experience long enough for the spark to fade. The world is always being explained (picas, pounds and quarks). Which strikes me silent, my mouth a hole some small creature digs in the middle of a lawn.

✦

The word is *stretcher*, not *bed*, let's get it right, *unconscious*, not *asleep*. The OR slopes just a bit, the doctor off in the corner counting his fingers. The nurse, barely a spectre of a being, promises prayer. Who do I talk to when I can't talk anymore?

✦

Here I am, Timbuktu again, the meaning of life a million fables away, still trying to listen to that inner voice, the fella with a trick tongue, the *Yum* in love with pretty much everything from honey to gravel. I love bungalows and kittens and whatever I can find in my fridge. I do my best to stay awake. Another orgasm, sure, okay. Nothing quite like a good conversation.

✦

I've been living with the little stranger for so long, I've given him features and a wardrobe, perhaps even a backstory. I call him *crony* when I've had a brandy or two. And then one day, feeling ancient or ill, I spot his shadow slithering across the blue vines of my bedspread. He's finally freeing himself from all my inattention. For a moment, I'll mistake him for the end, until one more time he corrects me, *Beginning*, one tiny blink between now and again.

A Numbers Game

Up to my elbows in twenty dollar bills,
charity work, not wealth, raising funds
for book bags and pre-school programs,
a kind of unselfishness that secretly
pines for payback of another sort,
a prime literary award, or a stranger
slowly becoming less strange
with every kiss. Wouldn't it be easier
to just get a higher paying job,
plump up my own pocket?
How many twenties before I can afford
to look as young as the Queen, her three strands
of pearls polishing the folds of her neck?

On my seven thousand dollar way
to the bank, I picture an ice slick,
tires skidding into the ditch,
all that money fed to flames, a greenish
hue of smoke smearing an already dingy
afternoon. So much of what we cherish
is made of paper, cut-outs held together
by gobs of sparkly glue. Rich or poor,
we are all prone to dotted lines and crumples,
prey to wastebaskets and recycling bins.
The money on the seat beside me
even hums a little decomposing tune,
deflation with every spendthrift breath.

At least I make a teller happy, the one
brazen enough to lick her fingers between sums.
She imagines a fur coat, amoral, of course,
and long, meaningful mornings lying in bed
letting time rewind her. If we put
our fantasies together, we might go so
far as to rob the joint, crash our way
into the steely vault and stuff ourselves
with gleam. So what if we rip a bit, if

we crinkle. Can't desire be repaired
for a price? Look how lightly I'm tripping
towards the door, floating through the grey blur
like an elusive lucky number.

Shangri-La, 7 pm

The 2006 Griffin Awards

Chartreuse streamers and orchids as pale pink
as babies' thumbs, Shangri-La, a place where
you can pretend to be thud-free, even blessed.
Pretending is your only requirement, gussied up
in silks and blush, holding hugs just a beat
too long, whooping metaphors, listening for
the echoes across the room. You've kissed
three sets of full lips in the last five minutes,
the nerves on the tip of your tongue squirming.
You've laced fingers with so many happy fists
that your palm boasts a handshake burn.
Everyone is a potential saviour, lover, mystery
revealed. The lights are low, sunk in the crimson
of wine glasses, sipped until your throat
has that satiated glow. Here the shadows
are beaded butterflies, ornaments that mark
the metamorphosis of self. And feasting still
to come, mango swirls and chocolate feats,
then dancing until that clichéd dawn. Don't balk,
you high court poet, a good cliché is reassurance
that you're not alone, bumping up to the open bar,
knowing that your billowy sleeves were the right choice,
that inch by inch you're flooding over
into pleasure so intense it feels like belonging.
You're invited, says the invitation. Simply fact,
Shangri-La, 7 pm. Leave your loneliness at the door.
Wrap yourself in streamers peeled from chartreuse
trees. Drop your nostrils into drifts of orchid
dust, inhale the make-believe of bliss.

Pancake Tuesday

Pancake Tuesday, believe it or not,
a whole day named after batter, sizzle
and flip. You tip the glass bottle of
maple syrup and drizzle the dusk
with a sweetness more naked than
dinner is supposed to be, not
a hint of carrot or corn, just a few
side swipes of bacon grazing the rim
of the plate and a mug of milk
to wash the butter down your throat.
Laundry Friday — leap into heaps of
clean clothes, spreading your pheromones,
60 bucks an ounce. Sex Saturday —
add up the swoons, gadding all
your best friends to the moon and back.
Prayer Monday, a whack of forgiveness
for the madness of inattention.

Another dawn and it's Ash Wednesday,
all your deaths twisting up the chimney,
such a soft rain of what used to be bone.
Lying on the family room couch
watching the big screen TV do its
reality imitation, a little sick
to your stomach from last night's
sugar fest. You can't hear the furnace
chugging in the background, but it's there,
spending buckets of hot air. In a more
focussed life, you'd be looking forward
to Furnace Day, waving your hand-held
pilot light out the window, charring
tiny trenches in the snow. Imagine
the awareness, 365 different jolts.

Tomorrow is up to you, standing
on its tiptoes, desperate to be seen.
What about Blizzard Day, stirring

the blur into a frenzy and stealing
blindly back to bed? There are days that
need to fail, ones so frail they can
hardly bend. But then comes next, and next,
call it as you feel, Illusion Day,
Meringue Day, Lucky Number Day, hours
tumbling into place. And just when you find
yourself beginning to think of pancakes
again, the last Tuesday in February
rolls around, dripping sweetness in your face.
It's living the moment, according to Buddha.
The day slipping from your tongue
something made to be forgotten.

At The Herb Shop

Too many kinds of lavender to count:
Provence Blue, Ellagance Ice, Spanish Eyes, Purple
Ribbon. After awhile, rubbing all those leaves
between our fingers, our skin is a brand new perfume.
Mixed with mint and then oregano,
we stink in legendary ways —
undiscovered molecules secreted
in a corner of the chemical galaxy.
Never been breathed before, not even in the form
of an idea. We sniff our fingertips, the crowd
already fading, memory slowly going aloof.
I wonder if you're more pungent, almost steal your palm.
I like the way we smell, even that acidy trace of henbane
with a Green River parsley on the chase. And
the patchouli plant, almost incense,
a drop of it beneath our thumbnails, a good,
long suck. Buck up, nothing lasts, we both know that,
yet hold our hands to our nostrils like open tubes
of glue. Ah, valerian, vanilla grass,
verbena. We can no longer tell the difference
between a spurt and a smear, between your flesh
and merely mine. At the café, we'll add caramel
and coffee to the air, snatching the quick rush
of a swoon.

Cacophony

Ian McEwan in my knapsack,
bottle of water, pen, all the supplies
I'll need for a bus ride down Yonge Street.
Never thought of earplugs, or sunglasses,
things to shut out the world. Too
busy opening up the way a poet
should. Then, cacophony, a crisis
of cell phones — battle of the tunes —
followed by the kinds of conversations
that were once whispered in stairwells or closets:
All he wants to do is fuck me. An ambulance
screams in the window, the boy behind me
kicks, and behind him, the foil of a snack bag
is pilfered again and again. Another
cell phone assault — *Don't talk back to me* —
a screech of brakes, a squeal of strong perfume,
the boing and flash of a computer game.
The wide man beside me who's had enough
falls asleep mere inches from my shoulder,
leaking air. If only I could shut down,
hand in my poet's *Be Aware* badge,
turn McEwan into a page flipping machine.
When the driver shouts my stop, I stagger
to the front, throw myself against the door's
hard whoosh. Outside, traffic lights
are humming some mocking melody
as I fail to distinguish between red and green.

In The Sum Of Things

In the end, a broken furnace
is just a blip, one measly night
huddled around a heater, telling tales
of swooning temperatures and north winds
that goosebump your nipples
no matter how many layers of clothes.
What's so tough about the water heater
flunking next, a faulty pilot light, the bathtub
cold as an ex-wife? People are sticks
in Africa, blow each other up in Iraq.
You've got a second toilet when the main one
goes bonkers, and the bang the stove fan makes
ruins Chopin. Get over it! Baby girls are
tossed overboard in China, teenaged boys
wear bullseyes on the West Bank.
So what if a light bulb flickers or the back
deck sags. To hell with the frayed screen door
and its open invitation to anything with wings.
This is still an easy life. Sure, your left big toe
can hardly bend, but movement is overrated anyway —
especially if your TV works and your couch
is in one piece. Hold back when your heart
breaks, there's always Scrabble or yoga class
to rearrange the pain. And who cares about
balding, belching, blood pressuring, all those
nuisances, when a good conversation
can whisk you miles away.

.3.

The Path

There is a path.   There is always
one path or another.   This one
is sunk in sand, strewn with
rusty pine needles and planets of acorns

that have somehow lost their heads.
Here and there, hard-backed beetles
huddle under fallen maple leaves,
pretending to be dead.   And the blossomy

prints of horse hooves boasting
prance and vigour.   All we can do is
follow.   Thousands have been here
before us; *multitudes*, we'd say,

biblically.   We are at once
special and ordinary,
an orchid and a wild aster
sharing the same glass vase.

We busy ourselves being here, the least
we can do in return for vision.
Watching the way fallen trees
end up in each other's arms.

Watching sturdier ones with holes
in their trunks, entries to other worlds.
Are we seeing what we're seeing
because of skill or has energy made a choice,

rendering us helpless in the presence
of toadstools and lichen, of
crinkled ferns and small white berries
that may not even have a name?

Are we walking or being led?
Togetherness is strangely singular,

the path perfecting its arrow.
When a dog suddenly bounds around

the corner, he flings himself at both
our legs, his tail tying us into knots.
Even the squirrels have more courage,
hanging upside down, bouncing branch to

branch, defying our need to separate
relationship from play.   Come, let's
walk a little further, stopping
now and then to pet some moss

or flip a rock, expose its buried wonders.
There is a path.   This path
is everywhere, the sand adding
our footprints to its map of trails.

We've So Much To Learn

Our spouses take French classes
so they can be more conversational.
Parents stare at TV remotes
the way cavemen studied stones.
Lovers trail wet fingers over our ribs,
tracing the sure death of pleasure.

All this time we're stuck
to computer desks, striving
to make ourselves purely informational.
No time for becoming the poem,
so to speak — an artifact of illusion,
a deep breath sailing across the Ethernet.
No energy for letting *whatever* happen.

Our pets groom themselves
for the next family photo
while our busy bacteria create new
immunities. Our molecules swig toxins
like teenaged boys at their first party,
destination *drunk*. And so we think
of bed, another day's notch,
learning curves too high for sheep to leap.

But who has time for sleep when there's
another *choose me* note to write, another
splinter of jargon to nail down,
another stage in the second hand's swirl.
Our spouses dream better mates.
Our cats purr the latest
incarnation of Bach.

We've so much to learn.
The future does its best to outlast.

The Trip

It surrenders with a highway,
the run-on sentence of the 401,
your long white leg as if glued to
the gas pedal.   There's no stopping
the idea of home once it pinpricks
a path into your head.   I think

comfort, familiar nouns and verbs
no more strenuous than *sleep* and *eat*.
I think *garden* and *fireplace*, both of which
deserve a bevy of adjectives
not found in this car.   Truth is, the trip
is already over, this is just

momentum winding down, making sure
muscles don't kink or memories sneak
out of the snapped shut camera.
These fields and forests are as far away
from destinations as the spires of clouds
glimpsed from airplane windows: no one

breathes out there, it's all dead scenery.
What probably isn't a hawk veers
into the blank-faced sky and disappears.
A service centre advertises
its fakery if fakery is what
you think you want.   All I want

is to stop thinking, stop feeling,
press the back of my skull into
the headrest, and be *there*, feet firm
in the puddles of my own driveway,
a *Globe & Mail* curled up and waiting for me
on the edge of the lawn like a basset hound.

There's A Moment In The Restaurant

There's a moment in the restaurant,
between the menu's flashy salesmanship
and the arrival (disappointment) of the food,
when you think you're going to faint. Hunger,
fatigue, fatal disease, you run through your options,
settling on denial, upright as usual.

You lift your tall, slithery glass of water
and roll the rim beneath your chin,
hoping to revive that earlier energy when the day
had legs. Another swirl down the drain,
another imbalance. No wonder you're so
light-headed, the list of non-accomplishments

terribly long. You didn't change your life,
for example, or your outlook, which is still
the same. You didn't water the coleus, or phone
the insurance company, or concoct a poem
out of yesterday's angst. There are unanswered
e-mails, shirts with missing

buttons in your closet, a garden shed
in desperate need of paint. All you did
was get yourself to this lousy restaurant
where boredom features prominently
with peanut stir-fry and the shrimp bouquet.
At least you'll eat.

You even count the number
of swallows per mouthful, go directly to obsessed.
Stop these silly attempts at steadiness,
let yourself fall. *Passed out today,*
you'll say, a mantra reminding you
of how human you really are.

Ha Ha

Halfway to the memorial: "Ha Ha!" scrawled across the dirty back
window of a van — the shock of seeing God's writing finger stiff as an
erection. The whole city sneering, *We're still here and she's not.* Coffee
cups loll in the gutters, crows spit from telephone poles, wire mesh
garbage cans bleed primary colours.

The sniggering van disappears and we slide into the parking lot like
actors taking stage direction — empty spaces with their dark osmosis.
Crematorium, now there's a word from the dictionary of bad intentions.
No way are we laughing this one off. *Entrance* glowers.

The performance continues as we scribble our little blue mark into
the guest book, handle a hug or two, pat our pockets for a rescue of
Kleenex. No wonder we feel so thready, so fly-in-the-web. The flower
arrangements look like after-images of fireworks, the minister fiddles
with her cross, the half-hidden boom box aches Billie Holiday-minus-
rehab.

Is this the best we can invent: a God who finger-paints neglected vans,
who hums huskily like heroin, who wads us up in his fist? "Ha Ha!"
the wooden box of ashes shouts, in a reprise of the cosmic joke. We'd
have to kill our brains to end this laugh-track grief, this knowledge that
the world blithely carries on.

Paradise

In paradise today, a wasp dunks itself
in my lemonade, tiny feeler-like feet clinging
to the inside of the glass, one dip away from
a drown. We are both blissing out on sugar.
He has a papery palace to sustain, a whole
community waiting to taste his version of this picnic.
While I head off on a mushroom hunt,
wildflower pluck, a dig for the right hunk of
quartz to feed the light on my window sill.

Hardly earth-shattering, these October afternoons,
pretending everything is a-okay. Not even thinking
of the unlucky ones who'll freeze in winter alleys,
who'll starve for national attention, quietly
drift away on a night so cold the very idea of warmth
has given up. With pumpkins on the front stoop
and rouged apples in our pockets,
we feel cozy, even safe.

And yet a sister wrestles with her third round
of chemo tomorrow. And once again
my lost friend won't call, fed up with expectations.
Plus, the usual humdrum: dusty corners, bills
collecting numbers, generic bad moods.
Just because it's pretty doesn't make a season
miraculous. The turkey in the freezer is,
after all, dead meat.

In a matter of weeks, the oak in my yard
will be boned and trembling. The rabbits
will have gone underground. Come frost
with its kill quotas, our rosy cheeks will take on
a rawness of fresh-spilled blood.
What an early-bird Scrooge. What's
the matter with me, unable to trade
my pessimism for one postcard photo?

Serves me right when my body leaves me behind,
legs out there on their own, kicking up a joy
of leaves, uncovering naked mushrooms, underbellies
frilled simply for the sake of tease. Toes wiggling,
soles pressing softness into every rock.

The Neglected Cottage

The place is a mess — peeled porches,
unraked leaves, towering weeds,
shingles curled at the edges like
villainous grins in silent films.
Branches flung across the property
as if the gods had had a fit. Jesus,
I'm pissed at the toppled clothesline, the caved-
in shed, the dock listing to the left.

Meanwhile, Christina grabs a rake,
scrapes the mashed fall leaves, creating
definition. Emilio tackles the water pump,
overpowering clutched clamps and
pouty plastic. And Karen, heroine
of a thousand previous invasions,
tries on all sorts of verbs: *scour, polish,
overhaul.* A red bucket of water beckons
from the porch, inviting immersion.

Day's end, muscles down
to their last penny, the place looks
rustic at worst, even picturesque.
So where's my relief, my happy?
Nowhere to store my angst, stuff
my insecurities. It's back to shouldering
the weight, wearing the sourpuss face.
Next to me the trees are lit with flounces
of sunset. A couple of chipmunks chase
each other through what little is left
of last year's leaves. I'm the odd one here,
the negative thought — the cloud
creasing the horizon.

The Night I Almost Choked

The night I almost choked on Tylenol,
a tiny voice swore it wasn't hard to die.
Just a caplet rolled to the back of my throat,
windpipe door wide open. A gasp
that any other time would have been a breeze.
Who knew that small could be hugely lethal?
At first I didn't say a word, panic
such a private place.   But what good are endings
without last words? *It's stuck*, I said, meaning
oh so many things.   Pointing at my Adam's apple
as if it were the first clue in a game of Charades.
What? someone said, shorthand for *Oh, bother.*
I was wrong, better to go quietly, let the blue
seep in like the Eastham tide, inch by
inch.   But the caplet budged against the flow
of a final swallow, a slow breakaway.
Now what to do, pretend it was nothing
but a blip? Cough to dramatize?
Or should I close my eyes, a lesser embarrassment?
The ghost of Tylenol pressing against my every breath
as if death had left the dent of its thumbprint.

The Empty Seat

An empty seat beside me
on the rattling subway, reminds
me of choosing sides in phys-ed class,
me always close to last with my
cowardly gangliness, wishing
the parquet floor would crack and reveal
a handy escape hatch.   Even then
I wanted to be wanted.   Are there nerdy
vibes still encircling me like the flies
haloing Pigpen's grimy head?

I can understand the fat guy
and his inability not to be intimate;
best he squeeze himself against the door.
But the middle-aged matron with
the Portugal-shaped mole on her cheek
and the yellow grocery bags knocking
her hips askew, is she afraid of me?

All around, people sway, willfully reckless
A twenty-something
boy whose pants are falling down, a wrinkled
businessman with a boulder of
a briefcase, a girl wearing wedgies
and hot pink socks.   How much I desire
them, the nerves in my right thigh pining away.
If only someone would bend towards me,
a waist dipping, a bum descending,

the beginning of a beautiful relationship.
The space beside me begs not to be a hole;
every second makes it steeper, wider,
more impossible to fill.   Teetering
on that edge, I hardly notice
the body slipping between
the boundaries, a slim Asian woman
dressed in black frills, a perfect fit.

Within seconds, she's sideways-reading
my book, quietly urging me
to turn the page. She's breathing in
on my out, like a teammate tossing me
the ball, pointing to the basket or
the pole, the exact place it belongs.
We ride together for several stops,
Summerhill, Rosedale, such dreamy-
sounding streets. And when she leaves me
at Bloor, an impression of her

remains, an indentation
in the cushion, a vague glimmer of
ruffled black light. There's enough fullness
to see me all the way to University.
When I stand, an entire Filipino
family fills my lack, kids on knees,
flesh overflowing. You'd never know
there'd been a rift, a leak of loneliness.
Walking away, I brush against
every shoulder, every open hand.

Christmas Spirit

This afternoon, I'm a substitute
for Father Christmas, the way Danzig
pretended to be Gdansk, a rope
of coloured lights slung over my shoulder
like fresh-killed rainbow. I've got ladders
and plugs and a few nudie balsams
dying to be adorned. I've got reams
of carols, the ones the angels used to
door-to-door when I was still patchy
as a glue-gun wreath. I've got stamina
and stretch, and a box of spare bulbs
that stare up at me like doll's eyes
pleading for a new face. And so
I drape and wind, I decorate.
There are antic elves between the boughs,
I'm sure of it, hauntings of Dickens-like
dementia. Tiny beams of fairies too,
their flickering bums stripper-sliding
down my arms. All the pulsing ice,
the reindeer reds, the low-price pinks.
No wonder I can't find Christ anywhere,
not even in the old robin's nest
curled up on a bed of dead fleas.
I've got sparkles and frost-lines and
bloody sugarplums, but no one to
save the day. It isn't the same without
a kid around. Ah well, the house
is finally flagrant, that's what really
counts. When I hit the switch,
the world explodes into a gaudy
mixed-drink womb.

Visitations

A fumble of childish knocks at my door,
conditional yet eager, a matched
pair of anxious smiles
that know anything to do with soul
is a serious affair. Jehovah's Witnesses.
Could Jesus have become
a timid middle-aged woman named Pat
after all these years? Is everything truly
possible, or is that just a huge
cosmic excuse?
A shudder in North Korea makes me
want to open wider, but my left foot
takes over, a wedge between two fears.
I smile like the damned do
when they're caught with holes in their hearts.
Sorry, I say, apologies for dead angels,
for physicists and their energy hives, for
a street still trembling with slammed doors.
Who would let God into their house
knowing how uncivilized He can be?
The Boy Scouts, the Avon lady, the spiritual
brigade — a parade of temptations
to help us believe we're not alone.

Later that night, I fumble with my car keys
in a deserted parking lot, a shiver of danger
slipping through my chains. If fate were a mugger,
I'd gladly surrender my identity — my bracelets,
my brain cells, my photo I.D. But what if the villain
turned out to be Death himself, for whom trinkets
aren't enough? I'd stare at his full-body frown
the way North Koreans watched their nuclear haze,
knowing that nothing would ever be the same again.
Where's Pat when I need her? Some spiritual intervention?
I knock on the car door lock, praying for luck,

praying to be safe behind the wheel again, back
in control. Death left behind with an oil slick
and the scent of burning rubber.

Home for another bedtime, a fleeting sense
of safety as I wash and brush, the mirror
avoiding a full-on gaze, more than aware
a blue stranger lurks within.
But what did Pat see when I creaked open
my front door, what did God glimpse
with His trespass glare?   An energy
on the verge of exploding?   Unhappiness
contaminating everything it looks at?
I see soul like a little smear of steam, breath
being all there is to the trick.
I see a man who still longs for salvation,
a transformation that can bend reality
into a brand new plan. *Anyone there?*
It feels like I'm touching the final flesh,
and being touched.
If a door were suddenly slammed,
I'd lose so much more than fingers.

The House Poems

Cold Kitchen

What a winter it's been, cold creeping through cracks in the sliding glass doors like a dictator wannabe, bananas shivering in their sallow skins, casseroles blue at the core. The angel of nourishment has been standing on the hot air register since November, blessing bags of frozen peas from a distance, dreaming of butter melting on the counter in slick pools of fallen light. How can the spirit feed in a roomful of zeroes, teeth sinking into icy holes? You mope in a straggly terrycloth robe, breathing in coffee fumes like oxygen, wondering what the world can mean when it's playing dead, wrapped in cellophane in a corner of the freezer.

Bedroom Mirror

You wake up to God getting naked in the mirror, robes slipping from his sloped shoulders. A good lesson in self-love. Admire the dimples in his knees, the spray of hair about his nipples, the mushroom at the tip of his cock. Feel the softness of his skin — quick! — before it sheds. You wish the world would evolve into eternal nakedness, chins and bums and pink flesh under pink nails, everything revealed. You tingle as you watch God wink away his hazel eyes, your own blues filling in the blank space with a thousand blinks.

Bathtub

A shine or two glistens across the tiles, the smell of lavender swirls from a bottle, a paperback with the picture of a beach on its front cover waits on the rug. You sink into the tub the way you'd let yourself fall into the arms of a saint. Doubt and anything else that might get in the way dribble down the drain. You are cradled from head to toe, caressed, made much of, explored from crease to pore, healed of all the strains of being human. A current of music skims through the open window, July with her uvula trembling. You press even deeper into those holy arms and sing along, bubbles of your breath rising to the surface in perfect oval arks.

Furnace Again

From the manger straw in the bricks of your foundation to the nails piercing October to the quick, you can't help seeing Jesus in the flames, the furnace door swung wide enough to squeeze your own sorry bones between the clouds of smoke, join the saviour as he roasts. So much love, it's unreal. Seems like the entire world has burst into orange and red, is bleeding glory into the air itself. You throw open your arms, embracing as much as possible. The chimney howls with a certain passion and the trees get naked even though they know they'll freeze. You and Christ fill the entire house with heat.

The Future

The donuts are doing their best gooey;
the coffee is an oil spill.
An ordinary meeting room heavy
with paper lassitude and fluorescence
weighs more than eggshells. We're here to talk
business, *retention* and *expansion*, which
conjures up diagrams in medical books,
bladders flexing their raw-red walls. The town's
future is at stake, growth potential,
a little village of mushrooms burgeoning
into infestation, free space gobbled up.
All we seem to talk about is years away,
our children's reign, a reminder of how
quickly we become defunct. Here and now
nothing but a starting gate, a pistol
raised, the first syllables in a brand new
Once upon... Who can blame us for not
listening to these hyper visions of
stretched highways and statistics dressed
in neater uniforms. We won't have a chance
to partake, six feet under by the time
time arrives. Will anyone remember
the afternoon we first agreed
when was the most important word?
Planning, such a soulless act, renaming
loss a relocation, replacing
anonymous committees with even
more distant hypotheses. How can we
be real enough to pare the sentence down,
to swear ideals are just a footnote away?
What I'd like to do is eat a donut
slowly, sip some cold coffee until I can
thoroughly describe the tastes. (Anyone
interested in the orgasm I had
last night, the shiver that branched all the way
up to my chest?) But the moment passes
and the emptiness needs to be surveyed.

Someone pours another cup, someone draws
a black line across a page. A 5-year
strat plan, 10-year projection,
25-year dream. Time travel in a bone machine.

A Conversation Is Rare

After listening to the phone not ring for hours,
a new sort of sensory deprivation,
I head outside in search of stimuli, something
to talk back to me, the terrier across the street,

the sum of his yips and nothing more,
or one of those yellow finches riding the remnants
of last year's daisies, teaching me the art
of soliloquy. I'll even chat to driveway gravel,

ask what it's like to just lie there and glint.
A conversation is rare and should never be judged
by its lack of sentience. Take this crabgrass
on my lawn, unaware no doubt of its weediness,

but still tenacious, a voice created from will and dirt.
And I swear the newborn forsythia is lip-synching
opera, the joys of being gold for an instant.
I walk the neighbourhood conversing, no need for

the cold silence of a cellphone in my back pocket.
A fly buzzes in my ear, sheer irrelevance,
the truth of most things. A clutch of violets
simmers, purple an act of eloquence and pomp.

Burbling, the whole of Holland Landing assures me
I'm not as alone as I think. What does it matter
if the crumpled coffee cup understands me, if
the cracks in the sidewalks are incapable of love?

Essence is all that matters, a soap bubble oblivious
to everything but its ability to float. I stop
and let my hand prattle to the black and white cat
out for a wander, a corresponding purr

trimming silence so softly even a feather
would leave a bruise. Is that a phone ringing
in the distance or a puff of air? Tell whoever it is
I'm too busy with the moment to talk.

Acknowledgements

I am indebted to the editors of the following magazines and anthologies who gave many of these poems a boost: *All Rights Reserved, Bei Mei Feng, The Best Canadian Poetry in English 2008* (Tightrope Books), *Bywords, CV2, The Dalhousie Review, Existere, Grain, The Malahat Review, The Nashwaak Review, The New Quarterly, nth Position, paperplates, Prairie Fire, Queen's Quarterly, Saranac Review, Scrivener, Studio, A Verdant Green: A Poetry Anthology to Celebrate the Lives of Anna And William McCoy, Wascana Review,* and *White Wall Review.*

Thanks to the Ontario Arts Council and the Canada Council for financial encouragement.

Deep appreciation to my Wednesday evening writing group: Sharon Wilston, Carol Gall, Hyacinthe Miller, Brian Dundas, Mike Madill, Elaine Rodaro, Richard Rodaro & Denise Raike; my Toronto poets' group: Maureen Harris, Maureen Hynes, Jim Nason, and Liz Ukrainetz; and my Newmarket group: Glenn Hayes, Angela Cherubini & Tara Stevens; and Joy McCall, whose amazing faith in my work crosses the ocean on a daily basis.

Thanks to the Richmond Hill Library, especially Laurie Valentine, for giving me a home away from home.

More thanks to Carolyn Marie Souaid who gave generously of her energy, editorial skill and ability to hear the music; Karen Haughian for making a dream a book; and Casey McGlynn for the incredible cover painting.

And absolute gratitude to Karen Dempster for putting her spirit and her love into every line I write. *Ooh, you make me live...*

About the Author

Barry Dempster is the author of fifteen books, including a novel, *The Ascension of Jesse Rapture*, a children's book, two volumes of short stories and eleven collections of poetry. He has twice been nominated for the Governor General's Award and has won the Petra Kenney Award, the Confederation Poets' Prize, the *Prairie Fire* Poetry Contest and the Canadian Authors' Association Jack Chalmers Award for Poetry for his 2005 collection, *The Burning Alphabet*. In 2009, he published two new books of poetry: *Love Outlandish* (Brick Books) and *Ivan's Birches* (Pedlar Press). Senior Editor at Brick Books, he has been a Wired Writing and Writing Studio mentor at the Banff Centre, and the facilitator of a two-week poetry master class in Santiago, Chile. He lives just north of Toronto, where he runs a film series and two book discussion groups.